How Can

I Be

Blessed?

THE CRUCIAL QUESTIONS SERIES
BY R.C. SPROUL

WHO *Is* JESUS?

CAN I TRUST *the* BIBLE?

DOES *Prayer* CHANGE THINGS?

CAN I *Know* GOD'S WILL?

HOW SHOULD I *Live* IN THIS WORLD?

WHAT DOES IT MEAN *to Be* BORN AGAIN?

CAN I BE SURE *I'm* SAVED?

WHAT *Is* FAITH?

WHAT CAN I DO *with* MY GUILT?

WHAT *Is the* TRINITY?

WHAT *Is* BAPTISM?

CAN I HAVE *Joy in* MY LIFE?

WHO IS *the* HOLY SPIRIT?

DOES GOD *Control* EVERYTHING?

How Can I Develop a CHRISTIAN CONSCIENCE?

WHAT *Is the* LORD'S SUPPER?

WHAT IS *the* CHURCH?

WHAT *Is* REPENTANCE?

WHAT IS *the Relationship between* CHURCH AND STATE?

ARE THESE *the* LAST DAYS?

WHAT *Is the* GREAT COMMISSION?

CAN I *Lose* MY SALVATION?

HOW SHOULD *I Think about* MONEY?

HOW CAN *I Be* BLESSED?

ARE PEOPLE *Basically* GOOD?

CRUCIAL
QUESTIONS
No. | 24

How Can
I Be
Blessed?

R.C. Sproul

ℝ *Reformation Trust*   A DIVISION OF LIGONIER MINISTRIES, ORLANDO, FL

How Can I Be Blessed?
© 2016 by R.C. Sproul
Published by Reformation Trust Publishing
A division of Ligonier Ministries
421 Ligonier Court, Sanford, FL 32771
Ligonier.org   ReformationTrust.com

Printed in North Mankato, MN
Corporate Graphics
July 2016
First edition

ISBN 978-1-56769-694-3 (Paperback)
ISBN 978-1-56769-695-0 (ePub)
ISBN 978-1-56769-696-7 (Kindle)

Cover design: Vanessa Ayala
Series template design: Gearbox Studios
Interior design and typeset: Katherine Lloyd, The DESK

All Scripture quotations are from *The Holy Bible, English Standard Version*, copyright © 2001 by Crossway Bibles, a division of Good News Publishers. Used by permission. All rights reserved.

Library of Congress Cataloging-in-Publication Data

Names: Sproul, R. C. (Robert Charles), 1939- author.
Title: How can I be blessed? / by R.C. Sproul.
Description: First edition. | Orlando, FL : Reformation Trust Publishing, 2016. | Series: Crucial questions series ; No. 24
Identifiers: LCCN 2016013793 | ISBN 9781567696943
Subjects: LCSH: Beatitudes--Criticism, interpretation, etc.
Classification: LCC BT382 .S67 2016 | DDC 241.5/3--dc23
LC record available at https://lccn.loc.gov/2016013793

Contents

One—THE BEAUTY OF BEING BLESSED 1

Two—BLESSED ARE THE POOR 9

Three—BLESSED ARE THOSE WHO MOURN 13

Four—BLESSED ARE THE MEEK 19

Five—BLESSED ARE THOSE WHO HUNGER 27

Six—BLESSED ARE THE MERCIFUL 35

Seven—BLESSED ARE THE PURE IN HEART 41

Eight—BLESSED ARE THE PEACEMAKERS 47

Nine—BLESSED ARE THE PERSECUTED 53

Chapter One

THE BEAUTY OF
BEING BLESSED

I once walked into my office to find a letter from a former student who was getting married in California and had invited Vesta and me to participate in his wedding. Our schedule prohibited our accepting, so he had written to ask, "If you can't come to our wedding, could you please record a benediction for our wedding?" I was moved by this request, and immediately a producer and I went into a recording booth and recorded a special prayer of blessing for this couple's wedding. I am sure I was far more moved by it than they were, because, as a pastor, I see pronouncing the benediction as one of the highest privileges that we have.

The word *benediction* simply means "good saying." It comes from two Latin roots: *bene*, meaning "good," and *dictio*, meaning "statement" or "saying." A benediction is a good statement, an announcement of blessing. The standard Old Testament benediction is the Aaronic blessing, found in Numbers 6. It is given in a poetic, parallel form:

The Lord bless you and keep you;

the Lord make his face to shine upon you and be gracious to you;

the Lord lift up his countenance upon you and give you peace. (Num. 6:24–26)

This standard Jewish benediction has three lines, and each line says the same thing in two different ways. In this kind of literary parallelism, if we fail to grasp the meaning of it in one line, the subsequent lines make it more clear so that we'll fully understand what's being expressed.

Notice also the emphasis on the face of God. This benediction is alluding to a special kind of blessing, a face-to-face intimacy with the Lord. For an Israelite, the highest state of happiness, the supreme experience of blessedness, was associated with coming as close as possible to the Creator, standing in His immediate presence, and basking in His unveiled glory.

The Israelites, as a semi-nomadic people, were acutely conscious of the fragility of human life. They saw that life seems to be like grass that sprouts and quickly withers and dies. They yearned for a permanent home. They wanted to be preserved. This benediction must have been tremendously encouraging. When it talks of the peace that the Lord brings, it's referring to something much more profound than cessation from military conflict. It's talking about an enduring peace, the peace with God that every soul hungers for. This benediction is the promise of the blessedness of peace, grace, and perseverance.

Throughout biblical history, this concept of blessedness was closely linked to the vision of God. What was referred to as a benediction in the Old Testament was sometimes called a "beatitude" in the New Testament. In this booklet, we're going to look at a famous and beloved portion of the New Testament that speaks about what it means to be blessed. This passage is known as the Beatitudes. It is part of the great sermon preached by Jesus Christ known as the Sermon on the Mount, and it is found in Matthew 5.

To understand the Beatitudes, we must understand a bit about the form they take. They are what are known as "oracles." What often springs to mind when we hear that word is something like the famous oracle of Delphi. This was a woman, a priestess at the temple of Apollo, who would look into the future and read the fortunes of kings and generals as they prepared for battle. She was called an oracle because she delivered a message from the gods; she was a conduit for divine revelation.

In the Old Testament, the prophets of Israel were agents of revelation. They did not speak their own message or express their own opinions but prefaced their teaching with the phrase "Thus says the Lord." Then they delivered a pronouncement from God. God said to Jeremiah that He would put His word into his mouth, and Ezekiel had to swallow the bitter scroll that became sweet to his taste, because it was the word of God.

In the Old Testament, *oracles* came to refer to divine pronouncements. There were two kinds of oracles: oracles of weal, which were announcements of prosperity or divine benevolence, and oracles of woe, which were pronouncements of doom or judgment. For example, Amos delivered a series of pronouncements prefaced by statements such as "Woe to those who are at ease in Zion, and to those who feel secure on the mountain of Samaria" (Amos 6:1). The negative form of the oracle in the Old Testament was often prefaced by the word *woe*. We see this also in Isaiah 6, where Isaiah got a glimpse of the inner court of heaven and saw the Lord exalted on His throne. Isaiah saw the seraphim flying about, singing, "Holy, holy, holy." His impulse on that occasion was to pronounce an oracle of doom upon himself, saying, "Woe is me! For I am lost" (Isa. 6:5).

This oracular form of address was also used by Jesus as part of His prophetic role. He pronounced oracles of judgment against the scribes and the Pharisees. "Woe to you, scribes and Pharisees, hypocrites!" (Matt. 23:15). In particular, Matthew's gospel records a great number of these oracles of doom.

The opposite oracle, an oracle of weal, was prefaced by the word *blessed*. The Beatitudes are a series of just this kind of oracle. Jesus was delivering the word of God to define the new covenant—the new situation that came to pass with His appearance.

The Beatitudes have two emphases. The first is the kingdom of God. This idea is central to Jesus' teaching, particularly His parables. John the Baptist appeared on the scene saying, "Repent, for the kingdom of heaven is at hand" (Matt. 3:2). Likewise, Jesus inaugurated His public ministry with the same announcement (Matt. 4:17). He frequently explained aspects of this kingdom by telling a story or relating a parable, prefaced by the phrase "The kingdom of heaven is like . . ." (see Matt. 13).

Even a cursory glance at the Sermon on the Mount and the Beatitudes reveals that Jesus associated the kingdom of God with His own life and ministry. We can't separate the person of Christ from the content of the Beatitudes, because the Beatitudes themselves point to Him as the ultimate source of our blessedness.

The Beatitudes are so called because they begin with the word *blessed*. There is a related expression that is used in theology with respect to this type of blessing. It has to do with the supreme hope of the Christian life. This hope is the beatific vision.

The beatific vision is the promise that, in our glorification, we will see God as He is. One of the most difficult aspects of being a Christian is loving, adoring, serving, and obeying a God whom we've never seen. We have to walk by faith, not by sight. Yet, the promise is given to us in the New Testament that there will come a time at the consummation of the kingdom of God when God's people will see Him as He is, in all His glory.

The reason this is called the beatific vision is because when we have that privilege of beholding God, the fullest aspiration of our humanity will be made complete. This hope is expressed in the famous prayer of Augustine of Hippo: "Oh God, You have made us for Yourself, and our hearts are restless until they find their rest in You." Even though the Christian life is to be marked consistently by a pattern of joy, as we move from joy to joy there is always a limit to the joy that we can experience in this vale of tears—and the total fullness of that joy will not be experienced until we see Him face-to-face. We will move then to a whole new level of personal satisfaction, of personal joy and fulfillment—in short, true blessedness.

This kind of blessedness penetrates into the deepest chamber of our souls, and it overwhelms the soul with a sense of sweetness, delight, satisfaction, and contentment that knows no bounds. It's this kind of blessedness that we will consider as we study the Beatitudes.

Chapter Two

BLESSED ARE
THE POOR

"Blessed are the poor in spirit, for theirs
is the kingdom of heaven." —Matthew 5:3

If you live in the United States, you don't live in a monarchy. As part of our national heritage, we Americans take pride in our representative form of government. Yet, we can't escape our fascination with monarchy. Fairy tales, nursery rhymes, and our preoccupation with British royalty all show that monarchy is still in our veins. We still think in terms of kingdoms. After all, most nations throughout world history have been ruled by monarchs.

The reign of God in Scripture is expressed in the language of monarchy. God doesn't rule by referendum; His commandments are not suggestions. He gives royal decrees, and He has elevated His Son to the position of King of kings and Lord of lords. The consummate form of government in this universe is a monarchy, for God has anointed His Prince to be our King. His Prince has the authority to bestow inheritance, membership, and ownership in that kingdom to whomsoever He chooses.

Notice that in the very first Beatitude, Jesus declares a promise regarding God's kingdom. The promise is that the kingdom of heaven will be given to those whom Jesus defined as "poor in spirit."

Immediately, a question arises. The gospel of Luke contains a sermon similar to the Sermon on the Mount. It is found in Luke 6, and it's sometimes called the Sermon on the Plain. In Luke's version, Jesus says simply, "Blessed are the poor" (Luke 6:20), omitting "in spirit." He also delivers a series of woes, including "Woe to you who are rich" (Luke 6:24). Luke's account contrasts "the poor" with those who, because they find their sufficiency in their wealth, are in grave danger of missing the kingdom of God. The question is, why is the qualifying phrase "in spirit" present in Matthew's account?

The point is not to exclude material poverty from this Beatitude. Rather, Matthew wanted his readers to understand that material poverty does not exhaust the meaning of this text. Those who are poor in terms of material possessions may be poor in spirit as well, but those who are wealthy may also be poor in spirit. There may also be deeply impoverished people who are bitter, covetous, or angry with God and are anything but poor in spirit. So we have to be careful not to make a direct identification between material poverty and spiritual poverty. The point is that Jesus is making a promise to those who are not rich in their own conceits but who find their sufficiency and satisfaction in God.

Jesus was addressing an issue that was anything but abstract to the people of His day. He spoke to those who were impoverished by the world's standards—some because of oppression by a foreign government, some because they had forsaken the enticements of this world to follow Him. Perhaps He had in mind the lament of the psalmist who wondered why the wicked prosper and the righteous suffer (Ps. 73). As the Wisdom Literature tells us, we live in a topsy-turvy world, where some set their hearts on power, wealth, and material things, stopping at nothing to gain an advantage over others.

Jesus taught that this topsy-turvy world will be set right in the kingdom of God. He promised that His Father noticed their plight. For Jesus Himself was lowly, and He promised those who would forsake the riches of this world and seek the face of God that His Father would deliver them. To them is given the kingdom of heaven.

Chapter Three

BLESSED ARE THOSE WHO MOURN

"Blessed are those who mourn,
for they shall be comforted." —Matthew 5:4

My favorite author, Herman Melville, once wrote, "Not till we know, that one grief outweighs ten thousand joys, will we become what Christianity is striving to make us." I don't know what Melville was thinking when he wrote those words. Perhaps he was remembering those words in the Wisdom Literature that "it is better to go to the house of mourning than to go to the house of feasting" because "the heart of fools is in the house of mirth" (Eccl. 7:2, 4). Or perhaps, he was thinking of this Beatitude.

Since the Beatitudes are pronounced in such a terse form, their full impact and the depth of their implications are not always immediately clear to us. Much has been written about this second Beatitude. Some see it as merely a promise of comfort to those who experience grief. Others see a more spiritual dimension to it, specifically, a sense of grief or mourning over one's sin.

It's wise not to restrict its meaning to either of those possibilities, because there are different kinds of mourning referred to in Scripture. Obviously, there is that mourning that comes with the loss of a loved one. There is also that mourning of regret for what one has done, whereby, when the Holy Spirit convicts us of our sin, we are profoundly saddened and moved to sorrow for having offended God.

But there is still another kind of mourning that is more broad in its application—a mourning brought upon people who suffer the pains of persecution. Jesus talked about suffering that comes as a direct result of being identified with Him. The children of God are children of mourning. In this, we are like our Master. Jesus was called "a man of sorrows, and acquainted with grief" (Isa. 53:3). He mourned the loss of loved ones, as He did at Lazarus' death, but we also see Jesus mourning over Jerusalem. He cried out, "O Jerusalem, Jerusalem, the city that kills the prophets and stones those who are sent to it! How often would I have gathered your children together as a hen gathers her brood under her wings, and you were not willing!" (Matt. 23:37; cf. Luke 13:34). Jesus was deeply grieved by all of the pain that He saw in this world and also by the force and power of wickedness in this world. He understood what it meant to be a mourner.

The Old Testament speaks of mourning in many places. In Ecclesiastes, we read that there's a time to mourn (Eccl. 3:4). The Psalms contain many expressions of profound pain, particularly from the pen of David, such as when he cried, "I am weary with my moaning; every night I flood my bed with tears; I drench my couch with my weeping" (Ps. 6:6).

Israel's history is that of a nation acquainted with suffering. Because of its location, Israel experienced great turbulence, as it was continually fought over. This tiny nation was a pawn in the many conflicts of the ancient world. It was a land marked with blood, pain, and suffering.

And yet, it was the Promised Land, the land that God gave to His people. So the people that He had called out from the world were a people acquainted with suffering. It was part of their national destiny. In their religious expectations, therefore, was the future promise of comfort.

In Luke 2, we find the narrative of Simeon. He was an elderly saint who had been given a promise by God: "Now there was a man in Jerusalem, whose name was Simeon, and this man was righteous and devout, waiting for the consolation of Israel, and the Holy Spirit was upon him. And it had been revealed to him by the Holy Spirit that he would not see death before he had seen the Lord's Christ" (Luke 2:25–26). Simeon was not only just and devout; he was waiting for something—the consolation of Israel. This term does not refer simply to an event or an experience of comfort that the nation would enjoy. The "consolation of Israel" was understood to refer to a person. This is one of the little-known titles for Jesus in the Bible. The Messiah, who ministered to the poor, the wounded, and the grief stricken, is the embodiment of the Old Testament promises of God to His people that He would be their consolation. The Messiah in His ministry would bring comfort to those who mourn; He would bring rest to restless souls.

That's the ministry of God to His people. He promises to heal their broken hearts and restore their souls. That is what is in view here in the second Beatitude. Not because mourning is a joyful occasion; Jesus was not diminishing the pain and grief that are associated with mourning. The reason we are blessed in mourning is because God's people are promised the consolation of Israel. The pain is a blessing in disguise; blessed are those who mourn, because they shall be comforted by the consolation of God with us.

Everyone knows what grief and sorrow are; everyone has been to the house of mourning. Where will we go for comfort? What is our consolation? Jesus said to the people, "Come to me, all who labor and are heavy laden, and I will give you rest" (Matt. 11:28). These were the words of the consolation of Israel incarnate. That is the promise of Christ to all who look to Him in the midst of mourning.

Chapter Four

BLESSED ARE THE MEEK

"Blessed are the meek, for they
shall inherit the earth." —Matthew 5:5

The philosopher Friedrich Nietzsche once famously declared, "God is dead." In saying this, Nietzsche did not admit to belief in a deity. Rather, he meant that the *idea* of God is dead. Nietzsche believed that God only existed in the minds of His followers, who were then responsible for his death: "God has been the victim of murder, and we, as human beings, are the murderers." Without this belief to anchor people, there is no trust in a cosmic order or any basis for morality or values.

Nietzsche also said the fundamental drive that motivates the human spirit is the will to power, or the drive to achieve. He held up as the human ideal the *Übermensch*, or superman. In the wake of the death of God, the *Übermensch* emerges to create a new set of values, which are centered on this world, as opposed to the otherworldly values of Judeo-Christianity. The *Übermensch* is characterized as a person of great boldness and courage, unfettered by old-fashioned values and fully able to exercise his own will to power. This is what we were created to be and do, according to Nietzsche, but the otherworldly values of Judeo-Christianity—with their emphasis on meekness, humility, and love—have squelched and destroyed the human spirit.

It is significant that Nietzsche interpreted meekness as a weakness that was put upon the world chiefly through the teaching of Jesus. He saw meekness as the reason God died—because He was too weak to survive. When we look at the biblical concept of meekness, we see something radically different from what Nietzsche saw, and frankly something different from the view that many Christians tend to have as well.

The concept of meekness often conjures up a picture of someone who is a doormat for everyone, who is wishy-washy, who has no backbone, and who lacks the virtues that Nietzsche exalted, such as courage. But the Scriptures provide two examples of meekness in two of the most prominent people in the Bible. In the Old Testament, the man noted for his meekness was Moses; in the New Testament, the man most noted for His meekness was Jesus. It would be extremely difficult to find any two figures in the history of the human race who exhibited greater strength of character than these two men.

Moses was a leader whose courage was astonishing. God gave him the burden of leading the nation of Israel out of slavery. He stood face-to-face against the most powerful ruler of the ancient world, the Pharaoh of Egypt. He withstood the stormy assaults in the wilderness of the rebels against him. Yet in all of this, Moses was noted for his meekness (see Num. 12:3).

Jesus referred to Himself as "gentle and lowly in heart" (Matt. 11:29). Yet, He stood against the entire power structure of His day, resisting public opinion, resisting the political and religious authorities, and enduring unbelievable pain and torture at the hands of His captors. But in spite of His enormous strength and power, He was called the epitome of meekness. Obviously, then, to be meek is not to be weak; in fact, to be meek in the biblical sense necessitates a certain kind of inner strength that is exceedingly rare.

I once knew a young man who was elevated to the position of leadership in an organization, and most of the people he led were older than he was—so the style of leadership that he adopted was one of a kind of tyranny, where he was officious and demanding, insensitive, and even brash. I asked him why he had adopted this particular style, and he said, "Because they won't follow me in my youth. I have to be strong or I will lose the power that I have with my office." I replied, "The more power that you have in this world and the more authority that has been given to you in any situation, the more necessary it is to be gracious and humble." This is a primary biblical teaching. It is easy, when one is in a position of power or authority, to use it in a display of arrogance and tyranny, but God resists that sort of style.

I told this young man that there is a strange secret that

many people don't get: not only is it important for people who are in positions of power and authority to temper that power with grace, but it's easier to be gracious when you have power. Because you have the power to be gracious, you don't need to be tyrannical. It's only when people are not secure in their authority that they manifest a kind of tyrannical reign over other people's lives.

That's important to remember when considering Moses and Jesus. No one in the Old Testament was endowed with more power than Moses was. And certainly, no one has ever had more power than Jesus had. Yet, with the grand scope of power and authority that these two men had, both understood that they could afford to be gracious. So, when Moses was described as being meek, in part what that means is that he wielded his power with gentleness and sensitivity, just as the Lord did.

Think for a moment about Jesus' leadership style. A person who is in charge of people must know them, realizing that some of them are stubborn and need to be prodded occasionally, while others are weak and wounded and need to be treated gently. This is what we see with Jesus. When Jesus dealt with people in authority, such as the Pharisees, He was stronger than steel; He took nothing from them, and He rebuked them with strong words. Yet, it is said of Jesus that "a bruised reed he will not break" (Isa. 42:3; cf. Matt. 12:20). With the downcast and the lowly of His day, He was tender, soft, and gentle. He was meek—that is, He tempered His power and His authority according to the needs of the people under His care.

The opposite of meekness is an arrogant, rough handling of power and authority. So often, when we think of people who wield power without any respect or regard for the people under their authority, the word that comes to mind is *ruthless*. The ruthless person does whatever it takes to achieve whatever he wants, and he is unafraid to use excessive force or power to accomplish his goals. It is difficult to be restrained when one has authority and power and one's vested interests are being threatened. When we want something and we know we can get it if we exercise power, then to step back and think of others and not of ourselves is being meek.

The man who is meek before God and has that inner strength that enables him to be gentle before men will not be a violent man. This quietness of spirit will enable him to be temperate. A self-controlled or temperate person is not given to binges of excess, but lives within restraints. Ultimately, the one who is meek submits himself to the authority and rule of God. Rather than trusting in his own abilities and authority, the meek one trusts that God will safeguard him and will fulfill His promises.

God has promised an inheritance to His people from the very beginning. The covenant that He made with Abraham involved land. In the New Testament, we are told that God is going to usher in a new heaven and a new earth. That's part of the broader promise of the kingdom of God. Jesus told His disciples to look for that day when the King will say, "Come, you who are blessed by my Father, inherit the kingdom prepared for you from the foundation of the world" (Matt. 25:34). God has promised the whole world as an inheritance to Christ, and those who are Christ's participate in that inheritance. So the meek person, instead of snatching or grabbing to possess what he can conquer in this world, is patient to wait for the inheritance that God promises.

We all need to search our souls when we hear these virtues set forth by Christ; none of us is as meek as we ought to be. Sometimes we confuse being meek with being weak. Sometimes we don't say anything when we should, we excuse our cowardice by attributing it to humility or meekness. Moses was not a coward, and certainly Jesus was no coward. Meekness does not preclude boldness, but it does preclude arrogance. The Christian who is meek is bold in being obedient to the call of God on his life. Ultimately, to be meek is to be submissive to the rule of our King.

Chapter Five

BLESSED ARE THOSE WHO HUNGER

"Blessed are those who hunger and thirst
for righteousness, for they shall be satisfied."
—Matthew 5:6

There's something strange about American culture. It has to do with our spirit of open and free competition. Competition is a necessary ingredient for the production of excellence. In the business world, for example, when one company has a monopoly, the tendency is for the work there to become sloppy and shoddy, because there is no competition to keep the company on its toes. The more competition there is, the more we reach down deep within ourselves to improve, to try harder, to do better.

When I did my graduate work in the Netherlands back in the 1960s, there was a terrible housing shortage. The Netherlands was the most densely populated nation in the world, and it was nearly impossible for a foreigner to find a place to live. I went from housing bureau to housing bureau trying to find an apartment for my wife and daughter. During this time, I learned my first Dutch idiom: *niets aan to doen mijneer*, which was always accompanied by a helpless shrug of the shoulders. It means, "There's nothing we can do about this." It drove me crazy, because I thought, there's always something we can do about it—that's the American way. The U.S. Army Corps of Engineers has a saying: "The difficult we do immediately; the impossible just takes a little longer." That's American ingenuity—the drive to succeed, to find a solution to problems. It wasn't until I lived in a different culture that I realized by contrast how deeply rooted that attitude is in American culture.

American people are mesmerized by competitive sports. I find myself caught up in watching football games, with my adrenaline flowing, and I'm nervous, wondering how it's going to come out. In terms of eternity, what difference does it make who wins a football game, and why should I be this concerned about it? If someone came from another planet and watched this, they would think we're crazy.

But what's important is the drama in the pursuit of a goal, the drive for success. We are goal-oriented people. It's in our blood, our traditions, our history, and our culture. Even the person who slaves all week long and doesn't feel like he's getting anywhere can at least have the vicarious thrill of seeing his favorite team succeed. Notice how we speak when we talk about our favorite sports teams: when the team wins, we say, "*We* won"; when the team loses, we say, "*They* lost." We want to participate in success. We want to win.

Some years ago, I spoke with a man whose business was to help people plan for the future. He asked me about my goals, about what I wanted to accomplish in life. As I went through this exercise, I noticed that one thing was conspicuously absent from my goals: there was nothing there about righteousness.

I thought, "What's wrong with this picture? How could a Christian establish life goals and not have at the top the attainment of righteousness in the sight of God?" Did not our Lord say, "Seek first the kingdom of God and his righteousness, and all these things will be added to you" (Matt. 6:33)? One of the scariest things that Jesus ever said was the warning He gave that "unless your righteousness exceeds that of the scribes and Pharisees, you will never enter the kingdom of heaven" (Matt. 5:20). The Pharisees were devoted to the quest for righteousness, but they ended up in a distorted pursuit of *self*-righteousness. It can be easy to dismiss the pursuit of righteousness as always ending in an inflated self-righteousness. But this does not eliminate the obligation that Christ gives us to seek first the kingdom of God and His righteousness.

This comes to the fore in the Beatitudes, where Jesus pronounced a blessing upon people whose goal is righteousness: "Blessed are those who hunger and thirst for righteousness, for they shall be satisfied" (Matt. 5:6). He didn't say, "Blessed are those whose goal is righteousness, for they shall attain their goal." Nor did He say, "Blessed are those who have a desire for righteousness, for they will get to their heart's desire." Rather, He spoke in everyday terms regarding intense hunger. We are not simply to seek righteousness or have righteousness as a goal; we are to hunger and thirst after righteousness.

Sometimes we see athletes who are so well paid that they tend to rest on their laurels and don't have a drive to win. Sometimes the critics will look at these superstars and say, "They're not hungry," whereas the young player who's not established and doesn't get the big bucks is hungry. He's giving 100 percent of his effort. When someone is passionately committed to his task, we say he's hungry for it. Jesus was not saying, "Blessed are those who are concerned in a cavalier way that they might, perhaps, grow in righteousness." He pronounced blessing on the ones who are hungry for it. Blessed are those whose thirst for righteousness is a consuming passion.

What does the New Testament say about Jesus Himself? That zeal for His Father's house consumed Him (John 2:17). This graphic language means that Jesus' passion for the affairs of His heavenly Father ate Him up. His food was to do the will of His Father. So Jesus Himself was pictured as a man who was passionately pursuing righteousness, and He achieved what He was pursuing. There's no way Jesus could have been any more righteous than He was, but He was hungry for it in His human nature.

We're conditioned to define ourselves in terms of our accomplishments rather than in terms of our character.

But Jesus pronounced blessing on a character trait: blessed are those who hunger and thirst after righteousness. He affirmed that this would not be a fruitless endeavor, for He promised, "They will be satisfied." Often, the teachings of Jesus, particularly in the Sermon on the Mount, echo sentiments that are found in Isaiah. In one place, God says this: "When the poor and needy seek water, and there is none, and their tongue is parched with thirst, I the LORD will answer them; I the God of Israel will not forsake them. I will open rivers on the bare heights, and fountains in the midst of the valleys. I will make the wilderness a pool of water, and the dry land springs of water. I will put in the wilderness the cedar, the acacia, the myrtle, and the olive" (Isa. 41:17–19).

This promise that God made, in a dry and parched desert land, was that He would fill those who are hungry and thirsty for Him. He said, "Come, everyone who thirsts, come to the waters; and he who has no money, come, buy and eat! Come, buy wine and milk without money and without price" (Isa. 55:1). We feed upon the bread of life, the bread that has come down from heaven, that nourishes the soul and fills the human spirit.

In the final analysis, we want the approval of God—but the applause of men can be deafening, and it can cause us to turn our attention toward achieving everything else apart from what Christ set as the priority for His people: to be righteous. Being righteous is not all that complicated; it means doing what is right. We have to have a passion to do what is right.

Chapter Six

BLESSED ARE
THE MERCIFUL

"Blessed are the merciful, for they
shall receive mercy." —Matthew 5:7

It's fascinating how the virtues in the Beatitudes are balanced with the promise that attends them. There tends to be a relationship between the virtue and the reward that is to be given to those who demonstrate that virtue. Those who hunger and thirst after righteousness are promised that they will be satisfied. Those who mourn are promised comfort. Those who are meek—that is, those willing to accept the providence that they have in this world—will inherit the earth.

In verse 7, there is the same kind of proportionality between virtue and promise: "Blessed are the merciful, for they shall receive mercy." This is both comforting and frightening. It is not an unusual teaching from Jesus; He taught this sort of thing frequently. Even in the Lord's Prayer, we are taught to pray, "Forgive us our debts as we also have forgiven our debtors" (Matt. 6:12), and later in the Sermon on the Mount, we're told that the same measure by which we are merciful to others is the measure we can expect God to be merciful to us (Matt. 7:2). This is frightening because we tend not to be as merciful toward others as God is toward us.

Jesus illustrates the link between showing and receiving mercy in the parable of the unforgiving servant (Matt. 18:23–35). A man was indebted to his master for more than he could ever possibly pay, and so he begged his master for mercy. His master had pity and forgave the debt. But then the servant turned right around and demanded from another man what he was owed, a very small amount of money. In this parable, Jesus shows the incongruity of receiving a tremendous amount of divine mercy while being miserly in dispensing grace and mercy on a human level. The promise of mercy is often linked to the command to be merciful—and we who have received the greatest mercy from God are the ones who should be the most merciful toward others.

In the gospel of John, we find the story of the woman caught in adultery (John 7:53–8:11). The Pharisees took this woman in her total shame and embarrassment and dragged her into the temple. Their concern in this encounter had nothing to do with their zeal to maintain the purity of the law of Moses; they only wanted to trap Jesus, and this woman was just a pawn. Under Old Testament law, adultery was a capital offense, punishable by stoning, to be administered by the religious authorities. But the Israel of Jesus' day was a conquered nation, occupied by Rome. One of the things that the Romans imposed upon conquered nations was Roman jurisprudence with respect to capital crimes: only Roman authorities could issue the death sentence and carry out an execution.

Here's the trap: if Jesus were to say that the woman should be killed in order to uphold the Mosaic law, then the Pharisees would go to the Roman authorities and say that He was disobeying Roman law regarding capital punishment. But if He were to say not to execute her, He would be setting aside the commandments of the Jewish law, and the Pharisees would denounce Him as a heretic.

At first, Jesus didn't respond. Instead, He started writing in the dust. John doesn't tell us what He wrote. Then He said to them, "Let him who is without sin among you be the first to throw a stone at her" (8:7). Then He stooped down and wrote on the ground again. One by one, beginning with the oldest, the crowd dispersed.

It's significant what Jesus did next. The woman had sinned, and Jewish law said to kill her, but Roman law said the Jews couldn't kill her. The Son of Man had more authority than Moses and more than the emperor of Rome; if He wanted to execute this woman, He had the authority under God to do it. He did not ignore the Mosaic law. He agreed that her offense was a capital crime. And He appointed her executioner: "him who is without sin." Was there anyone in that group who was without sin? There was one: Christ Himself. He had the authority and the power to execute that woman, and He didn't do it.

In the end, Jesus was left alone with the woman. He said to her, "Woman, where are they? Has no one condemned you?" (v. 10). And she said, "No one, Lord." And Jesus said to her, "Neither do I condemn you; go, and from now on sin no more" (v. 11). He did not declare her innocent or tell her not to feel guilty. There had been real sin, and Jesus didn't treat that sin lightly. But He addressed her with dignity and treated her with gentleness, kindness, and sensitivity. She was broken and humbled before Christ. He didn't give her justice; He gave her mercy.

There are many occasions when we quickly, abruptly, unthinkingly reach for the stone pile, forgetting that we are not without sin. Jesus was without sin, but instead of administering justice to this woman, He administered mercy. This story is a microcosm of how we all are in the presence of God, because we have all committed adultery in the sight of God. By worshiping other gods, we have betrayed our Beloved. The church is the bride of Christ, and the church is an adulterer.

The only way we can hope to stay in His presence is if He deals with us in the same way He dealt with that woman. He was merciful, and it's because of His mercy that we can live at all. It's by the grace of God that we continue to breathe in this world. That's why Jesus said, "Blessed are the merciful, for they shall receive mercy." It should be easy for us to be merciful, because we live every moment of our lives on the basis of God's mercy.

Chapter Seven

BLESSED ARE
THE PURE IN HEART

"Blessed are the pure in heart, for they
shall see God." —Matthew 5:8

In chapter one, we mentioned the supreme blessing that is
promised to every Christian, the beatific vision, in which
we will behold God as He is. We live our lives *coram Deo*,
before the face of God, but His face remains always invisible
to us. This Beatitude specifically promises the beatific vision.

Once again, we see that there is a connection between
the promise and the particular virtue exhibited by those to

whom it is promised. Those who are merciful will receive mercy. Those who are mourning will be comforted. Those who hunger and thirst after righteousness will be satisfied. Now, we are told that those who are promised the vision of God are those who are "pure in heart."

This is a scary statement. If God were to shine a spotlight on our hearts, He would not find hearts that are pure. If only those who are now pure in heart have any hope of seeing God, then we will be shut out. It is not because of a lack of physiological equipment, but because of the lack in our character.

Jesus said that those who are pure at their very core are the ones who will see God. In 1 John, we see the promise of the beatific vision: "See what kind of love the Father has given to us, that we should be called children of God; and so we are" (1 John 3:1a). John introduced this section of his epistle with an expression of Apostolic amazement. The thing that is so incredible and astonishing is that people who are not pure in heart are adopted into the family of God. We simply do not qualify for that relationship in terms of our own character; nevertheless, we are called the children of God.

John goes on to say: "The reason why the world does not know us is that it did not know him. Beloved, we are God's children now, and what we will be has not yet appeared; but we know that when he appears we shall be like him, because we shall see him as he is. And everyone who thus hopes in him purifies himself as he is pure" (3:1b–3).

People often have questions about what things will be like in heaven. What will we be like? Will we know each other? Will we appear to be the same age that we were when we died? Or will we have glorified bodies that somehow are ageless? How will we occupy our time? We are always puzzled by these things, and John was puzzled too, for he said, "What we will be has not yet appeared." We are given glimpses of what heaven will be like, but we don't have a complete picture of what to expect when we cross over to the other side. John was cognizant of the limits of our knowledge, and even the limits of the revelation that he received about these matters from the Lord, but He doesn't leave us groping in the darkness. We don't yet know what we will be like, but this much we do know: we will be like Him, that is, Christ.

Elsewhere, when the New Testament speaks about the consummation of Christ's kingship at His return, it uses the language of *apocalypse*, which means "unveiling." At this point, Christ will be made manifest; He will appear in His full glory. When the Bible speaks about seeing Him again, we are told that when He appears in this unveiling, we will see Him; every eye will behold Him. So the force of these passages should direct our attention to the hope of seeing Christ in the fullness of His glory.

The theological definition of the Trinity says that the Father, the Son, and the Holy Spirit are three in person, but one in essence or being. This truth promises something even greater, if that's conceivable, than seeing Christ face-to-face in the fullness of His glory. We won't simply see the expression of the perfect image of God; we will see God in His very essence, face-to-face. Obviously, this poses a difficult philosophical and theological question: If God is a spirit, how can the Bible speak of seeing Him in the purity of His essence, when His pure essence is spiritual and invisible?

Jonathan Edwards had some interesting thoughts on this question. His thinking is certainly speculative, but it gets me excited when I think about it. We put great stock in being an eyewitness; someone will say that something is true because he saw it with his own eyes. We know how important physical sight is, and what a blind person would give to have his sight restored. So, we must have functioning eyes to see, as well as a brain that correctly interprets the images. But the ability to see is not enough; we need light. We can't see in the dark. Edwards suggested that the experiences that we think of as direct and immediate eyewitness experiences are really indirect and mediated experiences. They pass through the intermediate steps of light, sensation, nerve stimulation, and so on. According to Edwards, the ultimate vision of God will be one that takes place without the eyes. It will be a direct and immediate apprehension by the human soul of the very essence of God—a completely and dramatically transcendent mode of perception. All of the barriers that prevent our seeing God will be removed, and we will be filled in our souls with direct, immediate apprehension of the being of God.

Jesus said, "Blessed are the pure in heart, for they shall see God." The thing that keeps us from having the vision of God now is our impurity, our sin. John said that when we see Him, we will be like Him, for we shall see Him as He is. The question remains as to whether God will glorify us in heaven, allowing us to see Him as He is, or whether He will show Himself to us, which will purify us. We don't know the answer to that, but it's interesting to think about, because nothing would be a greater agent of purification than a direct, immediate vision of the nature of God. John said that even the promise of this future vision works to begin our purification right now. So, keep it always in front of you as the ultimate promise for the fullness of your soul.

Chapter Eight

BLESSED ARE
THE PEACEMAKERS

"Blessed are the peacemakers, for they
shall be called sons of God." —Matthew 5:9

The making of peace is one of the most important motifs
of all of Scripture. In fact, the whole drama of redemp-
tion involves the pursuit of peace in the midst of a war that
spans the whole world and almost all of history since cre-
ation. In Genesis 3, we read of the fall of the human race;
this is not only an isolated historical event but the beginning

of a worldwide situation of hostility and estrangement. In the New Testament, the gospel is articulated in terms of reconciliation: God in Christ was reconciling the world to Himself, and we who believe in Him have been given a ministry of reconciliation (2 Cor. 5:18–20).

There are certain necessary conditions for reconciliation to take place in any dispute. The first is estrangement, because without estrangement there is no need for reconciliation. Gospel reconciliation is the healing of a broken relationship.

I once gave a lecture at a college to a group called the Atheist Club. The club had invited me to give the case for the existence of God. I had been studying a sermon by Jonathan Edwards titled "Men, Naturally God's Enemy," where he talks about the hostility toward God that is found in the human heart since the fall. The Bible says that the flesh is at enmity with God—that we are, by nature, enemies of God (Rom. 8:7). The thrust of my lecture to these students was that the disposition of their hearts was one of hostility toward God. The problem was not that they didn't know God or were indifferent toward Him; their problem was that they hated God. I told them I was willing to discuss proofs for God, evidences of the resurrection, and so on, but that in the end they were dealing not with an intellectual problem, but a moral one. It wasn't for lack of evidence that they didn't believe in God; it was because they didn't want to. This reality is at the heart of the rupture between God and man.

Disputes and hostilities erupt in all kinds of human relationships. Husbands and wives who were once united in the holy bonds of matrimony sometimes become estranged. In the workplace, violent conflicts can arise between labor and management, resulting in strikes, acrimony, and dissension. One of the most powerfully felt needs in our culture is for whole relationships. Estrangement is not foreign to us. Often, these conflicts move us to see the need for mediation.

When labor negotiations break down, often an appeal is made for a mediator to try to lead the estranged parties into agreement. Marriage counselors and pastors often function as mediators between husbands and wives. A mediator is a go-between; he tries to speak to both sides in the dispute in order to bring them to unity so that the hostilities will stop, the breach will be healed, and reconciliation can take place.

This is why the heart of the message of Christianity is

a message of peace. The supreme peacemaker is Christ, because the supreme role occupied by Jesus in the New Testament is that of our Mediator. He mediates the estrangement between us and God. It's not that we have estrangement because God has turned His back on the human race, but because the human race has turned its back to God. But God has not washed His hands of us; God the Father sent Christ to perform the work of mediation, to be our peacemaker.

The language of peace is used throughout the New Testament to describe this event of reconciliation. When Paul wrote to the Romans about God's mercy, grace, and forgiveness in justifying unjust people through the work of Christ, he wrote, "Therefore, since we have been justified by faith, we have peace with God through our Lord Jesus Christ" (Rom. 5:1). Our ultimate peace has been secured for us by the supreme mediator, who Himself is the Son of God. Because of His mediatorial peacemaking, we are able to be adopted into the family of God. That's why Jesus said, "Blessed are the peacemakers, for they shall be called sons of God." Just as He is the Son of God and is the peacemaker, so those who are His, who imitate His office of peacemaking at an earthly level, will be called sons of God.

We can find several examples of peacemaking in the Bible. Joseph made peace with his brothers (Gen. 45), Jonathan interceded for David (1 Sam. 20), David sought to be reconciled to Saul (1 Sam. 24:8–15), and Paul confronted Peter over his hypocrisy in order to call him back to the gospel (Gal. 2:11–14).

Why are we not more involved in making peace? One of the main reasons we shrink from the task of being peacemakers is that it is a dangerous job. If you step in between two men in a fight, you might be the one who gets the next punch. And a peacemaker is a lightning rod; he tends to become the target of hostilities from both sides. If ever there was a thankless job given to a human being, it is peacemaking.

When Jesus pronounced His blessing upon peacemakers, He was pronouncing a benediction on people who work for authentic, genuine, godly peace—not for what Martin Luther called a carnal peace, a false peace. The false prophets of Israel boasted of their peacemaking skills; their favorite message was one of peace. The prophet Jeremiah, God's spokesman for reconciliation, mediated the word of God to a wayward nation and called the people back to Him. The people would not listen because they didn't like His prescription for peace with God. The false prophets would say,

"God's not angry, everything is OK. God loves you just as you are." Jeremiah went to the people and said these prophets cry, "'Peace, peace,' when there is no peace" (Jer. 6:14).

An authentic peace is hard to accomplish because it may require the call for repentance. That kind of peacemaking is very unpopular, and so it often meets stiff resistance. Jesus has to encourage us to be peacemakers because it may mean standing in harm's way—though not to the degree that Jesus did. He took upon Himself the fullness of God's wrath against man, as well as all the wrath man directs toward God; no human being has received greater hostility from the human race than Jesus did at Calvary. At the same time, He received the full measure of the wrath of His Father against sin. He took it from both sides. He did it in order to effect our peace.

Chapter Nine

BLESSED ARE THE PERSECUTED

"Blessed are those who are persecuted
for righteousness' sake, for theirs is the kingdom
of heaven." —Matthew 5:10

When I was a senior in seminary, I had the dubious honor
of being selected to preach the "senior sermon." Every
year, one member of the graduating class was invited to address
the whole student body, the faculty, and the entire assembly
of the local presbytery in a special convocation at the school.

The seminary I attended was not noted for its commitment to orthodox theology or conservatism, and I was often swimming against the current. In my sermon, I preached from the book of Job and talked about the nature of human sin.

In the course of my years in seminary, I had learned different ways to define and explain the nature of sin: in terms of the limitations of human existence, inauthentic existence, and the threat of non-being. All of those categories had some interesting insights, which I acknowledged in my sermon. But, I said, when I read the Scriptures, this is not the definition of sin that I find there. It's far more than being finite, inauthentic, or threatened with non-being. Sin, according to Scripture, is an offense against God, who is holy. I talked about Job's initial attempt to defend himself against the transcendent majesty of God; yet, when he saw God appear, Job said, "I lay my hand on my mouth. I have spoken once, and I will not answer; twice, but I will proceed no further," and "I despise myself, and repent in dust and ashes" (Job 40:4–6; 42:6).

My classmates warmly embraced me and expressed their gratitude for the sermon. It was an extraordinary experience of love and affection, but it was short-lived. As I left the chapel, three professors were standing at the doorway

with the dean of the institution, and they were obviously
enraged. They heard in my sermon a critique of the theology they had been teaching. The dean, trembling in anger,
came over and strongly rebuked me. With his finger in my
face, he said, "That was the worst distortion of Christian
theology I've ever heard."

Dr. John Gerstner was professor of church history and
theology and an expert on orthodox Reformed theology.
Still white and trembling, I went to his office and told him
what had happened. He looked at me with a warm smile
and said, "Blessed are you, Roberto" (which was his nick-
name for me, after the great Roberto Clemente). "Every
Reformed Christian from Martin Luther to B.B. Warfield
is rejoicing in heaven over the sermon that was preached in
the chapel of this institution this morning." He continued,
"Don't you realize that what you have experienced today was
being persecuted and slandered for the sake of the gospel,
and our Lord said, 'Blessed are those who are persecuted'?"

Living in America, we have the freedom to preach the
gospel without being exposed to violent criticism or persecution. This has not been the case for many Christians
around the world and throughout history. There's no question that the history of Christianity is filled with stories

of the persecution of God's people. Christians have been jailed, tortured, and killed, and have had their businesses, livelihoods, and reputations destroyed. Martin Luther was accused of stirring up a hornet's nest, creating so much conflict over the gospel that he should have been ashamed of himself. He said that anytime the gospel is preached clearly, without distortion, there is conflict, and if there is no conflict in the life of the church, it's probably a sign that the gospel is not being preached.

It has to be asked of our generation: Why are we not in jail? Why are we not being stoned and beaten with rods as the Apostles were? Why do we not have people gnashing their teeth at us with the kind of visceral hostility that Jesus and the Old Testament prophets received?

Of course, if people are angry with us, it doesn't necessarily mean we're being faithful to the gospel. It may be that we are being insensitive or offensive, and that people are reacting justly. And we must be careful here. We don't want to cause offense with our behavior; if unbelievers are going to take offense, it should be to the gospel message itself, which pierces unbelieving hearts. But it must be asked whether something is amiss when we do not face the kind of opposition that Christians have historically received.

One reason we don't face as much opposition is because the culture is more indifferent than it used to be. But perhaps the biggest reason for the absence of greater persecution in our day is that we have learned how to avoid it. We have become masters of conflict avoidance, and the best way to avoid conflict regarding the gospel is to water it down in order to make it more palatable to people.

I remember how surprised I was at the reaction of some of my friends to my conversion to Christ. I was converted in my freshman year in college; it was the most exciting event in my whole life, and I couldn't wait till the first break when I could come back to my hometown and see all my friends. We had known each other for years and loved each other. Yet, when I told them about my conversion, they looked at me like I had lost my mind. They said, "You're some kind of fanatic." Some of them even became hostile. I was shocked; I was happy to discover Christ, and I assumed they would be too.

I realized there was always the temptation to soften the call to repentance that God gives to all of us. The New Testament warns that we must beware of people-pleasers and those of whom everyone speaks well, because Jesus said,

"They hated Me and they're going to hate you." He didn't suggest that this was a possibility; He said it was a certainty: "In the world you will have tribulation" (John 16:33).

It is easy to become paranoid in response to the unpleasant experience of rejection. But we are told to look to God for the grace to endure persecution for the sake of Christ and His kingdom. Christ is honored when His people patiently bear the hostility of the world. We should not be surprised when these things happen, nor should we seek to make it happen. It goes with the territory when we are preaching the gospel and living for Christ.

In this last Beatitude, Jesus said that those who are persecuted for a just cause—persecuted for Jesus' sake—are going to receive the kingdom as their inheritance. As we are despised and rejected by men, as we experience hostility, we share in Christ's suffering, for He has suffered these things before us and for us. And the Father has made Him King of kings, and He has prepared a kingdom for those who walk with Him.

These believers—who identify with His rejection and who are patient and willing as their character is being developed through trials and through persecution—are, as the Apostle Paul said, filling up in their own lives the afflictions of Christ (2 Thess. 1:3–12). The response to being reviled and rejected by men should not be bitterness, not losing heart, and not being discouraged—but, according to Jesus, to rejoice and be glad.

The Beatitudes are God's prescription for how we can be blessed. They tell us what pleases Him. He delights to give to those who delight in Him and to comfort those who are in distress. He promises the world to those who submit to Him and imitate His gracious authority, and He promises to fill those who yearn for righteousness. Those who show mercy will receive mercy, and those who are pure will see God. Those who make peace are truly those who know peace with God through Christ, and those who are persecuted for Christ's sake will gain the kingdom. In all these ways, God promises to bless those who would seek Him. And one day, we will receive the ultimate blessing: to behold Him as He is, and to glorify Him forever.

About the Author

Dr. R.C. Sproul is founder and chairman of Ligonier Ministries, an international Christian educational and discipleship organization located near Orlando, Fla. He is also copastor of Saint Andrew's Chapel in Sanford, Fla., chancellor of Reformation Bible College, and executive editor of *Tabletalk* magazine. His teaching can be heard around the world on the daily radio program *Renewing Your Mind*.

During his distinguished academic career, Dr. Sproul helped train men for the ministry as a professor at several theological seminaries.

He is author of more than one hundred books, including *The Holiness of God*, *Chosen by God*, *The Invisible Hand*, *Faith Alone*, *Everyone's a Theologian*, *Truths We Confess*, *The Truth of the Cross*, and *The Prayer of the Lord*. He also serves as general editor of the *Reformation Study Bible* and has written several children's books, including *The Knight's Map*. Dr. Sproul and his wife, Vesta, make their home in Sanford.

Further your Bible study with *Tabletalk* magazine, another learning tool from R.C. Sproul.

....

TABLETALK MAGAZINE FEATURES:

- A Bible study for each day—bringing the best in biblical scholarship together with down-to-earth writing, *Tabletalk* helps you understand the Bible and apply it to daily living.

- Trusted theological resource—*Tabletalk* avoids trends, shallow doctrine and popular movements to present biblical truth simply and clearly.

- Thought-provoking topics—each issue contains challenging, stimulating articles on a wide variety of topics related to theology and Christian living.

Sign up for a free 3-month trial of *Tabletalk* magazine and we will send you R.C. Sproul's *The Holiness of God*

TryTabletalk.com/CQ